Hurricanes and Tropical Storms

Jennifer Nowak

Rosen REAL READERS

Rosen Classroom Books and Materials
New York

Published in 2002 by The Rosen Publishing Group, Inc.
29 East 21st Street, New York, NY 10010

Book Design: Haley Wilson

Photo Credits: Cover, p. 1 © Alan Klehr/The Image Bank/Getty Images; pp. 2-3, 14-15, 16 © Kaz Mori/The Image Bank/Getty Images; pp. 6-7 © BEST-BACKGROUNDS/Shutterstock.com; pp. 8-9 © NASA; pp. 10-11 © Harvepino/Shutterstock.com; pp. 12-13 © Bloomberg/ Contributor/Getty Images; p. 14 (inset) © Mark Winfrey/Shutterstock.com.

ISBN: 0-8239-8223-8
6-pack ISBN: 0-8239-8626-8

Manufactured in the United States of America

Contents

Wet and Windy Weather

A **tropical** (TRAH-pih-kul) storm happens when strong winds and rain begin over a warm ocean. During a tropical storm, winds can blow between forty and seventy miles per hour! If a tropical storm's winds blow faster than seventy-five miles per hour, it is called a hurricane.

The word "hurricane" comes from Spanish and Native American words for evil spirits and bad winds.

Where the Storm Starts

Tropical storms and hurricanes start in warm ocean waters around the **equator** (ee-KWAY-ter).

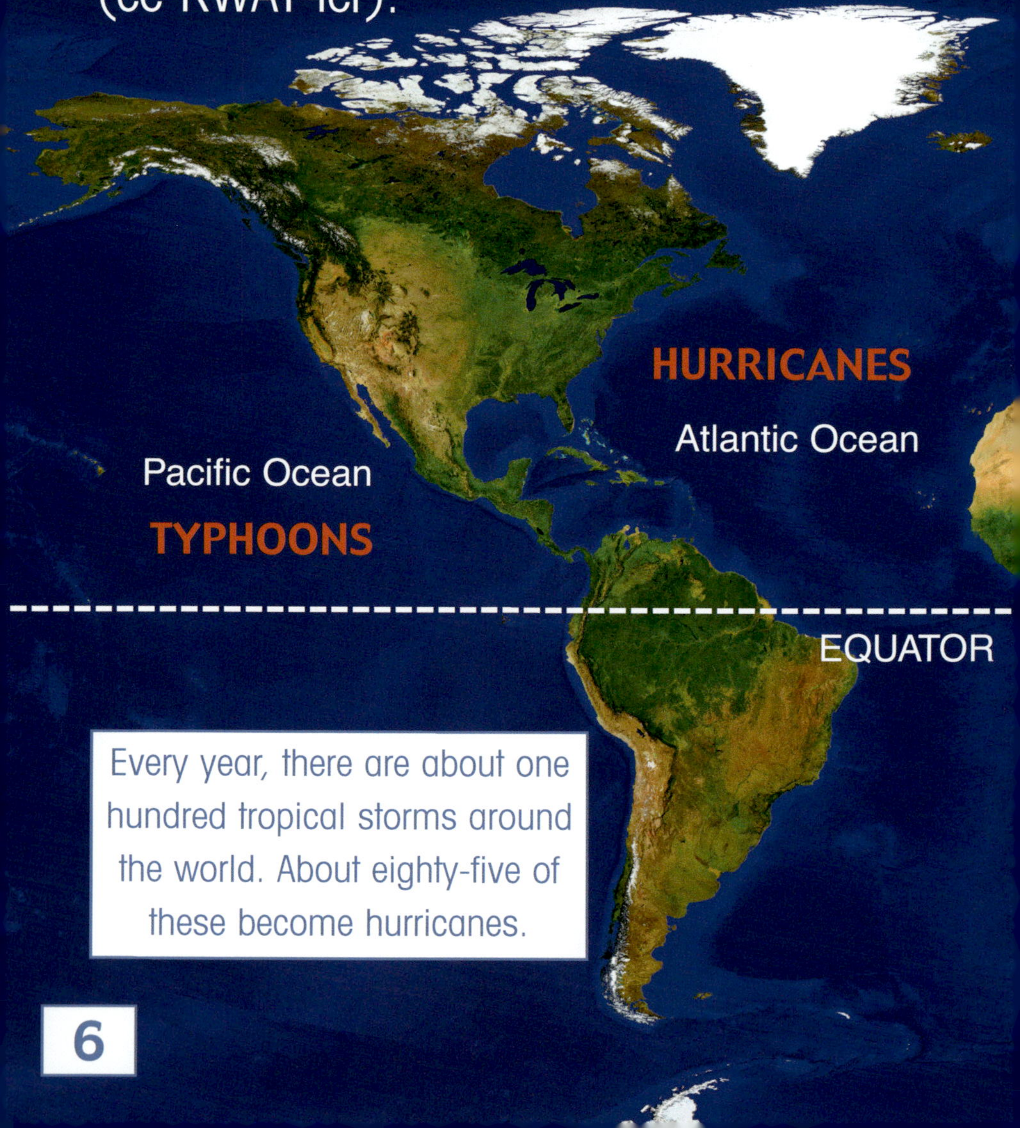

Every year, there are about one hundred tropical storms around the world. About eighty-five of these become hurricanes.

Hurricanes that happen in the Indian Ocean and around Australia are called **cyclones** (SY-clohnz). In the southern and western Pacific Ocean, they are called **typhoons** (ty-FOONS).

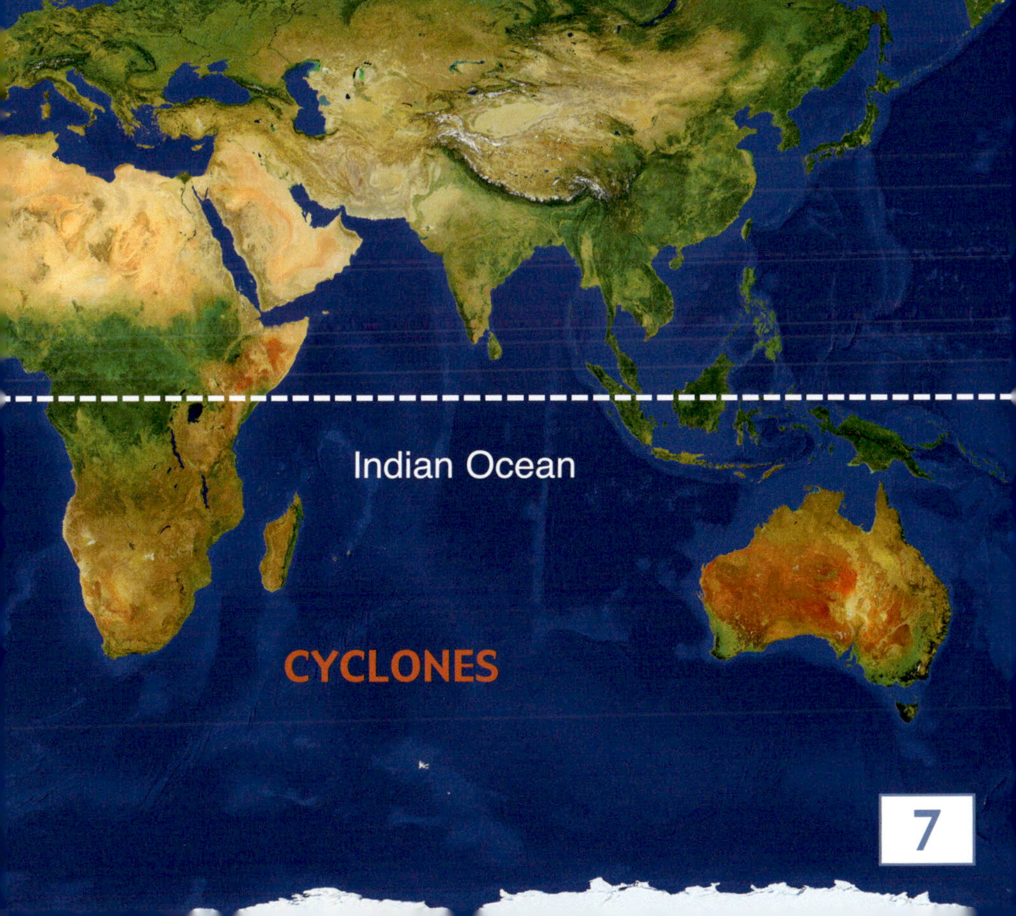

How the Storm Starts

Sometimes warm ocean water turns into clouds of warm, wet air. These clouds rise. More warm air rushes in to take the place of the rising air. A **column** of sinking air forms in the middle of the rising air. The winds begin to **swirl**, and a storm begins. The warmer the ocean is, the stronger the hurricane can be.

The center of a hurricane is called the "eye." The eye of a hurricane is always calm.

How Hurricanes Act

A hurricane spins and moves forward like a top. At first, a hurricane moves at about ten to twenty miles per hour. As it moves north, it can speed up to sixty miles per hour. When it moves over land, it loses strength because there is no hot, wet ocean air to keep it going.

Hurricanes are about ten miles high and can be hundreds of miles wide.

Danger!

Tropical storms and hurricanes can be **dangerous**. Heavy rains can cause floods. Strong winds can destroy buildings and blow things through the air. Storms also cause oceans to rise higher than usual. Huge waves can form and crash over land.

A tropical storm can cause floods strong enough to wash away homes!

Storm Safety

People who live in places where tropical storms hit should know which roads lead away from the water. They should have a lot of bottled water and listen to a radio for weather reports. When people are told to leave the area, they should leave quickly. You can stay safe during a tropical storm by following these safety tips.

Glossary

column	An object that is tall and thin.
cyclone	A different name for a hurricane.
dangerous	Not safe. Harmful.
equator	An imaginary line around the middle of Earth that separates it into two parts, north and south. Areas on or near the equator are always hot.
swirl	To spin very fast.
tropical	Having to do with a part of the world where it is hot and wet throughout the year. Tropical places are usually near the equator.
typhoon	A different name for a hurricane.

Index